Sophie Carter.

HOT TOPICS

DINOSAURS

Written by John Cooper

www.alligatorbooks.co.uk

Published by
Alligator Books Limited
Gadd House, Arcadia Avenue
London N3 2JU

Printed in China

Contents

What are dinosaurs?

An unusual early reptile was Longisquama which lived in Asia 240 million years ago. Only 15 cm long, its back carried a row of stiff, tall scales.

Dinosaurs lived millions of years ago. They were reptiles, a group of animals that today includes lizards and snakes, turtles and tortoises, crocodiles and alligators.

Q How many different types of dinosaur are there?

A Scientists have grouped dinosaurs into several sorts:

THEROPODS All the meat-eating, two-legged dinosaurs like Tyrannosaurus.

SAUROPODS The giant plant-eating dinosaurs like Apatosaurus and Diplodocus.

ORNITHOPODS Smaller, plant-eating dinosaurs which walked on two legs like Iguanodon, duck-billed dinosaurs, and hadrosaurs, such as Tsintaosaurus.

CERATOPSIANS The horned dinosaurs like Triceratops, all plant-eaters.

STEGOSAURS The dinosaurs armed with plates like Stegosaurus. They were plant-eaters and walked on four legs.

ANKYLOSAURS This group includes other armoured dinosaurs like Nodosaurus. Like the stegosaurs, they were plant eaters and four-footed.

PACHYCEPHALOSAURS The name means 'thick-headed' and describes a group of dinosaurs with very thick skulls, named after the best known, Pachycephalosaurus.

Q When did dinosaurs live ?

A Dinosaurs lived only during the Mesozoic Era or so-called Age of Reptiles. The Mesozoic Era lasted from 250 million to 65 million years ago. No-one has ever seen a living dinosaur. The earliest of human ancestors did not appear on Earth until 4 million years ago.

Q Were dinosaurs the first reptiles?

A Many other types of reptile lived before the dinosaurs. The very earliest reptile that scientists have recognised was found in Scotland in 1989 in rocks 335 million years old.

Tanystropheus was a 3 metre long early reptile which lived 250 million years ago. Its neck was incredibly long.

The sprawl of an early reptile (left) and the upright legs of a dinosaur (right).

Q Where did the dinosaurs come from?

A Fossil evidence shows that a group of reptiles living in Argentina about 230 million years ago developed a new way of walking.

Instead of walking with sprawling steps like crocodiles, they began to walk with their legs more directly under their bodies, like the dinosaurs. One reptile, called *Lagosuchus*, may have been the ancestor of all the dinosaurs.

Q How do you tell the difference between dinosaurs and other fossil reptiles?

A Two important things make a dinosaur. First, they all lived on the land. Second, they all walked on upright legs. All other reptiles, whether fossil or living had different ways of moving.

Q Did all the dinosaurs live at the same time?

A The dinosaurs lived throughout the Mesozoic Era. Different sorts lived at different times.

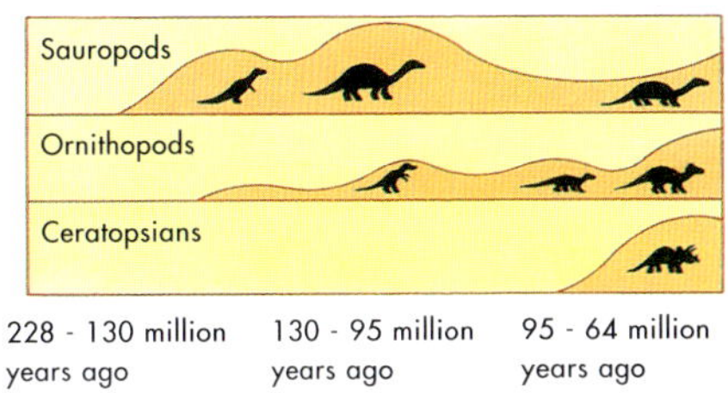

Q What was the very first dinosaur?

A What is believed to be the world's oldest dinosaur was found in Argentina in 1991. Named *Eoraptor*, it lived 228 million years ago. It was over one metre long, perhaps the size of a large dog. Other early dinosaurs have been found in South America and even older ones may still be discovered.

Plateosaurus has been found in western Europe in large groups of skeletons. They probably travelled in herds.

Where did dinosaurs live?

Plateosaurus

Dinosaur fossils have been found on every continent, even in Antarctica. But since dinosaurs first appeared on Earth, the positions of the continents have changed a great deal.

Q Did any dinosaurs live all over the world?

A No single type of dinosaur lived everywhere. Some groups of dinosaurs were more common than others. *Plateosaurus* belonged to a small early group called the prosauropods and close relatives have been found in the USA, Germany, South America and South Africa.

Q Where did *Tyrannosaurus* live?

A *Tyrannosaurus rex* is the one dinosaur everyone knows. But there are very few examples of skeletons and most are quite incomplete. They were all found in the USA, mainly in Montana.

Q Are dinosaurs found in every country?

A No, but they have been found in many. Famous finds have been made in what is now USA, South America, Canada, Tanzania, Mongolia, China, Australia and India, as well as many European countries.

The continents today are still moving. North America and Europe are drifting apart from each other about as fast as a fingernail grows.

Pachycephalosaurus and its relatives had skulls up to 25 cms thick on top! Scientists believe that head-butting contests were held to defend territory or for rivals to fight over the leadership of a herd.

Q How could the same dinosaurs live on different continents? Did they swim across the ocean?

A For many millions of years, they would not have needed to. The continents have been drifting apart slowly ever since they were formed. Today, *Brachiosaurus* can be found in two continents - Africa and North America. When *Brachiosaurus* was alive it was still all one continent.

Q Did dinosaurs have homes?

A The largest dinosaurs may have had favourite resting places on the edges of forests or beneath cliffs. The smaller dinosaurs could perhaps nestle in more sheltered spots safe from their enemies.

Q Did dinosaurs always live in one place?

A Some herbivorous dinosaurs may have migrated in search of fresh grazing.

Q Were the dinosaurs which lived in the Antarctic cold?

A The Earth's climate was much warmer during the dinosaur's reign. The continent we now call Antarctica was much nearer to the Equator. The dinosaurs would not have seen any ice-caps! Reptiles cannot survive very cold climates.

Which dinosaurs were found first?

When Gideon Mantell first showed his dinosaur teeth to other scientists of the day, they were identified as being from a rhinoceros!

Early in the nineteenth century, some strange fossils were found in southern England. They were recognised as being from creatures entirely new to science. No-one really knew what these creatures looked like.

Q When were the first dinosaurs found?

A Gideon Mantell, a doctor from Sussex, found the teeth of *Iguanodon* in 1822. In 1824, William Buckland described some bones which he called *Megalosaurus*, but found some years before. After these discoveries, many people began to hunt for the fossil bones of these new giant lizards.

Q Why didn't anyone ever find them before?

A We know that dinosaur bones were found but no-one realised that they had once belonged to huge extinct reptiles. One bone was thought to be from a giant man!

Iguanodon got its name because its teeth looked like giant versions of the living marine iguana from the Galapagos.

Q Why do dinosaurs have such funny names?

A Each dinosaur is given a special name using words made up from two ancient languages, Latin and Greek. The names usually mean something which describes the creature in some way. *Megalosaurus* means 'big lizard'.The same dinosaur names are used by scientists of all nationalities.

For hundreds of years, the Blackfoot Indians of Canada thought that the dinosaur bones they found were the remains of their ancestors!

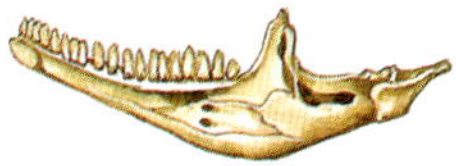

Dinosaur teeth have been collected by Chinese doctors for over 2000 years. They are believed to come from dragons and are ground into powder and used for medicines!

Q What did they think dinosaurs looked like when they first found their bones?

A Gideon Mantell drew the first reconstruction of a dinosaur in 1835. He first thought that *Iguanodon* must have been like a giant lizard 21 metres long. We now know that it is about 10 metres long. In 1854, several life-size models of dinosaurs were built in the gardens of Crystal Palace, London. *Iguanodon* is still there to-day, looking rather like a rhinoceros!

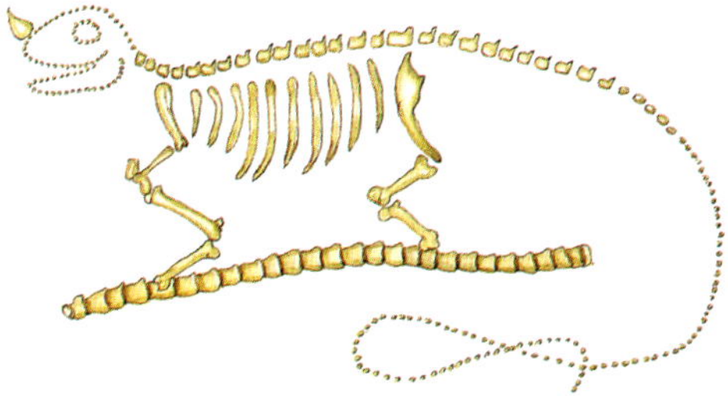

Q When was the first complete skeleton of a dinosaur found?

A The first was also one of the most spectacular finds ever. In 1878, almost 40 skeletons of *Iguanodon* were found in a coal mine in Belgium.

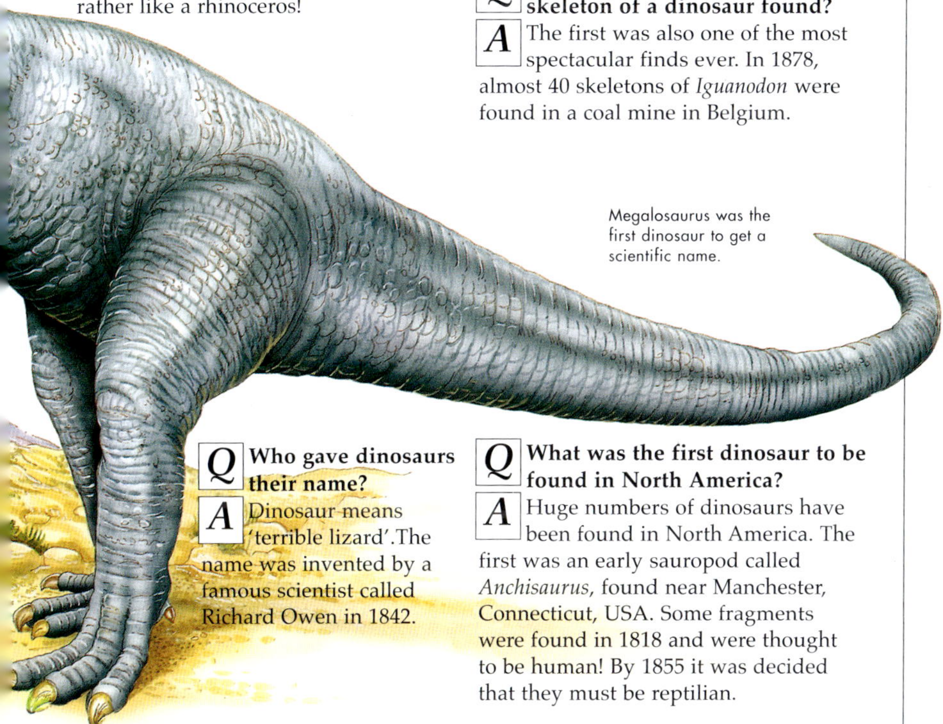

Megalosaurus was the first dinosaur to get a scientific name.

Q Who gave dinosaurs their name?

A Dinosaur means 'terrible lizard'.The name was invented by a famous scientist called Richard Owen in 1842.

Q What was the first dinosaur to be found in North America?

A Huge numbers of dinosaurs have been found in North America. The first was an early sauropod called *Anchisaurus*, found near Manchester, Connecticut, USA. Some fragments were found in 1818 and were thought to be human! By 1855 it was decided that they must be reptilian.

What did dinosaurs look like?

'Supersaurus' had a shoulder blade around 2.5 metres long!

When complete skeletons are found, scientists can be fairly sure that they can put the bones together in the right order. But could we guess what you look like just from your skeleton?

Q How do scientists know how to put dinosaur bones together?

A Scientists use their knowledge of other animals to put dinosaur skeletons together. But for a long time after dinosaurs were first discovered, many mistakes were made. *Apatosaurus* even got the wrong head for nearly 100 years because it was originally found without one!

Q Were dinosaurs fat or thin?

A It is difficult to tell if a dinosaur was fat or thin as fossils are usually just the remains of their hard parts - normally bones and teeth. Modern plant-eaters such as elephants, hippos and cattle have big stomachs - and plant-eating dinosaurs were probably just as big. Smaller, more agile dinosaurs needed to be slimmer to move quickly. Scientists and artists have to use comparisons like this to get an idea of how each dinosaur might have looked.

Early this century, some scientists thought that the legs of Diplodocus sprawled like a lizard. But its chest would have dragged along the ground!

Q What was the smallest dinosaur?

A Perhaps the smallest dinosaur was *Compsognathus*. Fully grown it was only 70 cm long and most of this was a long tail.

Compsognathus

Mamenchisaurus was 22 metres long but 10 metres of that was its neck! It lived in China 160 million years ago.

Gideon Mantell thought that an odd spike-shaped bone he found must be a horn on the nose of Iguanodon. It turned out to be a thumb!

Q What was dinosaur skin like?

A A few fossils of dinosaur skin have been found proving that the skin was

tough, dry, waterproof and made of small rounded scales. Sometimes there have been signs of armour plating.

Q What was the biggest dinosaur?

A The *Brachiosaurus* is the largest complete skeleton ever to have been found. It is 12 metres tall, 23 metres long and weighs 70 tonnes. The *Diplodocus* is the longest skeleton ever to have been found, at 27 metres long. But some new discoveries in Colorado and New Mexico might be from even bigger dinosaurs. '*Supersaurus*', '*Ultrasaurus*' and the largest '*Seismosaurus*' were truly gigantic. *Seismosaurus* would have been similar to *Diplodocus* but may have been over 36 metres long and weighed up to 130 tonnes! This would have been the biggest animal ever to have lived.

Q If no-one has seen a dinosaur, how can scientists be sure that they get dinosaurs to look right?

A We can never be sure what dinosaurs looked like. Scientists still argue about the way many dinosaurs might have appeared. Even well-known dinosaurs like *Iguanodon* can be made to look quite different when drawn in different poses.

Q What colour were dinosaurs?

A Even fossils of skin cannot tell us what colour it was. Modern reptiles, especially the lizards, have a wonderful variety of colours and patterns and dinosaurs may have been just as colourful. Bright patches of colour might have been important for the dinosaurs to recognise each other and to display warning signs. The large plant-eating dinosaurs were probably camouflaged. But would we have guessed at the zebra's stripes with only bones to study?

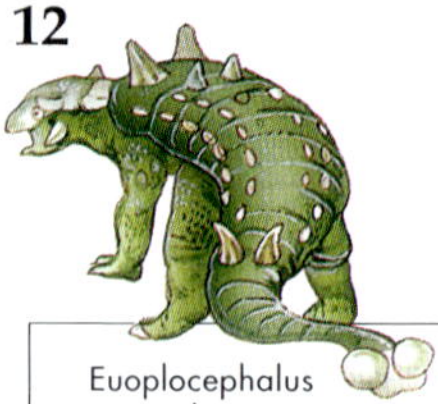

Euoplocephalus stunned its attackers with the bony club on the end of its tail.

What did dinosaurs eat?

Some dinosaurs had up to 2,000 teeth.

Some dinosaurs only ate plants. Other dinosaurs only ate meat. Plant-eating animals are called herbivores and meat-eating animals are called carnivores.

Q Which dinosaurs only ate plants?

A Most dinosaurs ate plants. The huge sauropods, the largest of all the dinosaurs, are the best known. They had long bodies, tails and necks, and small heads with special teeth for grazing. With their long necks they could reach up into trees.

Diplodocus

Dinosaurs never ate grass. It did not appear on Earth until after the dinosaurs had become extinct.

Q How can you tell what a dinosaur ate?

A Fossils of the teeth and jaws are the most important clues.

Narrow, curved, sharp teeth belong to the carnivores like *Tyrannosaurus*. Herbivorous dinosaurs have flatter, grinding teeth, like *Camarasaurus*, or sharp nipping teeth like *Iguanodon*. *Ceratopsians* had beaks to help tear off leaves.

Q How did dinosaurs protect themselves from attack?

A Many dinosaurs were protected by armour. This included hard plates, horns and spikes.

Stegosaurus

Plant-eating dinosaurs swallowed stones to help grind leaves up in their stomachs.

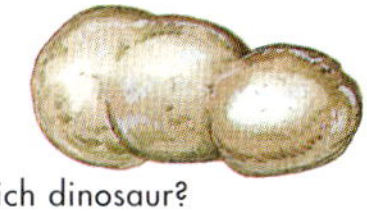

Fossils of dinosaur droppings have helped scientists discover what dinosaurs ate. But which dropping came from which dinosaur?

Q How did dinosaurs kill?

A Carnivorous dinosaurs had sharp claws as well as sharp teeth: both would have made good weapons. Some large carnivores, like *Tyrannosaurus rex,* may have used their heavy skulls as battering rams.

Q Did dinosaurs eat each other?

A Some carnivores were fast and would have chased other dinosaurs, perhaps even their own kind. They may have hunted in packs like hyaenas. Small *Coelophysis* skeletons were found in an adult *Coelophysis*. Large carnivores, like *Tyrannosaurus*, were too heavy to chase prey and perhaps fed off dead or slower moving dinosaurs.

Q How much did dinosaurs eat?

A Plant-eating dinosaurs ate most of the time to get enough nourishment. *Diplodocus* ate about a tonne of leaves a day! The meat-eating dinosaurs' diet was much richer so they did not need to eat huge quantities regularly.

Q What else was there for dinosaurs to eat?

A Small reptiles, birds, fish and insects were all food for the dinosaurs.

Tyrannosaurus rex's teeth were more than 15 cm long and very sharp for slicing and tearing at flesh.

No-one knows what Tyrannosaurus used its very short arms for as they did not even reach its mouth!

Tyrannosaurus measured 14 metres in length and stood almost 6 metres high.

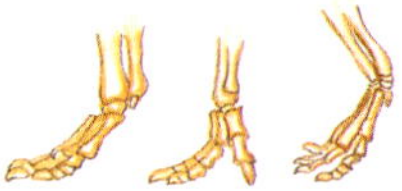

Could dinosaurs run?

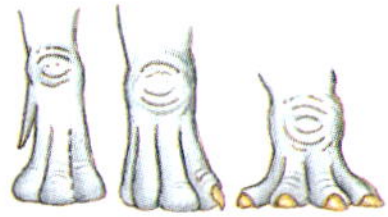

The arrangement of the bones in the ankles and feet of dinosaurs show that all except the sauropods and stegosaurs could run, and footprints prove that they did!

Dryosaurus

Ceratosaurus

Just as lions hunt zebras today, the meat-eating dinosaurs hunted the plant-eaters. The carnivores ran to catch - the herbivores ran to escape.

Q How fast could dinosaurs run?

A A trackway made by *Tyrannosaurus* shows that it could have outrun a charging rhinoceros, perhaps reaching 45 km/h. The fastest of all was a small two-footed dinosaur which left footprints showing that it could run at nearly 70 km/h. But we don't know which dinosaur it was! The great sauropod dinosaurs like *Apatosaurus* walked at a speed of only 5-8 km/h.

Q Did dinosaurs leave any other marks or prints?

A In only very rare cases, marks have been found where dinosaur tails dragged along the ground. Generally though, despite the enormous size of some tails, they were held up above the ground, and not just when running.

Q Could dinosaurs hop, skip or jump?

A Once, some footprints were believed to have been made by a hopping dinosaur but are now thought to have been made by a turtle swimming in shallow water. Footprints have been found showing a dinosaur with a missing toe, and another with a limp! Scientists believe that at least the active therapods could jump, but there is no evidence from footprints! Ninety-nine out of a hundred trackways show walking dinosaurs.

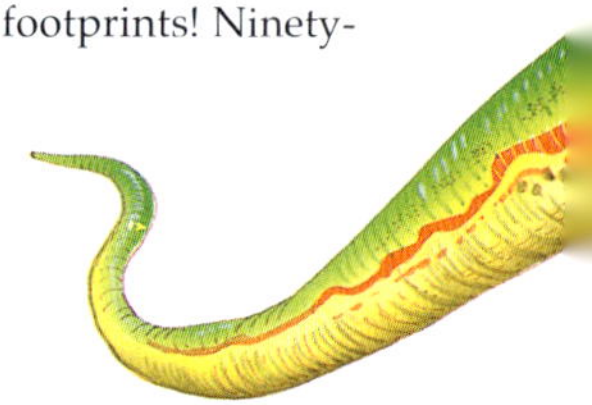

Fossil footprints give us clues about the shape of the foot as well as the weight and speed of the dinosaur. There are sometimes skin impressions too.

Though many dinosaurs could run well, they may not have been able to run for long distances before becoming exhausted.

Q Where are fossil footprints found?

A Throughout the world there are about a thousand places where dinosaur tracks have been found. One of the most famous is at the Davenport Ranch in Texas, in rocks 100 million years old. There, and in nearby places, thousands of footprints have been found.

Q Are there any footprints of young dinosaurs?

A One of the Texas trackways contains the footprints left by 23 sauropod dinosaurs which seem to have been travelling as a herd. Many of the footprints are quite small, probably belonging to youngsters. It is thought that the larger members of the herd travelled in front and at the sides of the herd, the smaller ones were protected in the centre.

Q How can footprints be fossilised?

A Dinosaurs crossing muddy lakes or sea shores left behind their footprints, just as animals do today. If the mud dries in the hot sun, the next tide or flood washes more mud into the imprints which are then preserved.

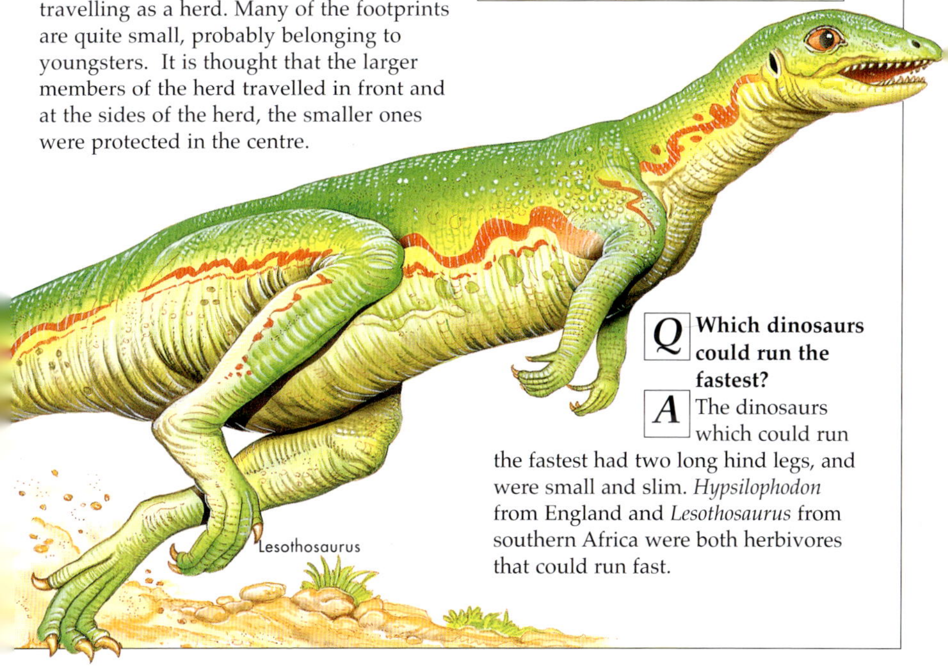

Lesothosaurus

Q Which dinosaurs could run the fastest?

A The dinosaurs which could run the fastest had two long hind legs, and were small and slim. *Hypsilophodon* from England and *Lesothosaurus* from southern Africa were both herbivores that could run fast.

Could dinosaurs swim?

Plesiosaurs have long necks, short bodies and large paddle-like limbs, rather like modern sea-lions.

Like any land-living animals today, such as elephants, hippopotamuses and buffaloes, the dinosaurs enjoyed a good paddle and swim too.

Q Were any dinosaurs amphibious?

A This was an old idea. It was once thought that the heaviest dinosaurs like *Brachiosaurus* and *Apatosaurus* were too large to support their own weight on land, and therefore had to live in water. Scientists have now calculated that their large leg bones were strong enough to support them out of the water.

Q If the Loch Ness monster really does exist, wouldn't it be a swimming dinosaur?

A If Nessie ever was found and proved to be a reptile, she would almost certainly turn out to be a plesiosaur, ichthyosaur or pliosaur. These were all marine reptiles and were not dinosaurs, which only lived on land.

Q Did any dinosaurs live permanently in the water?

A Probably not but ideas change. The long necks of dinosaurs like *Mamenchisaurus* were once thought to be useful for breathing in deep water. Unfortunately, water pressure at 10 metres or more would not have allowed the lungs to work.

Apatosaurus being chased by Allosaurus

Ichthyosaurs looked rather like modern sharks and dolphins.

Many modern creatures like dogs, elephants, polar bears and even cows can swim. They don't need flippers or webbed feet and dinosaurs may have been able to swim just as well.

Q Did the swimming reptiles live at the same time as the dinosaurs?

A Throughout the reign of the dinosaurs, the ichthyosaurs and plesiosaurs were very common in the seas and oceans of the world. There were many types, including the pliosaurs and elasmosaurs. The largest of all was an Australian pliosaur called *Kronosaurus* which grew as large as 13 metres.

Q Could dinosaurs float?

A Despite the enormous size of some, there is no reason to suppose that any dinosaur would sink. One set of brontosaur footprints shows only impressions from the front feet! It seems that the dinosaur was floating in a lake and simply kicked itself along with its front feet.

Q Could dinosaurs have fed under water?

A Water plants would have been good food. Dinosaurs with weak teeth like the ankylosaurs may have grazed rather like hippos or like ducks in shallow water.

The long hollow crest of *Parasaurolophus* was once thought to be a sort of snorkel used while feeding below the water.

Q Did any dinosaurs have flippers to help them swim?

A There may be one dinosaur that did. One species of *Compsognathus* found in Germany seems to have had flipper-like front legs. No-one is sure, but perhaps they allowed it to swim extra quickly to catch prey or escape from its own hunters.

Could dinosaurs fly?

Longisquama glided through the air with its long scaly wings.

Some small dinosaurs have skeletons almost identical to *Archaeopteryx* - the oldest known bird. The dinosaur ancestors of the birds must have developed the ability to fly or glide short distances.

Q How well could *Archaeopteryx* fly?

A Probably not very well. Compared to modern birds its muscles were weak and it was much heavier. But it could have flapped its wings quite well and its bony, feathered tail would have made a good rudder to help it manoeuvre on long glides through the air.

Q How did dinosaurs get feathers?

A Reptile scales like those on snakes and lizards may have become 'feathery' to help keep the smaller dinosaurs warm. Only later did they also prove useful for flying.

Q How did the dinosaurs learn to fly?

A Perhaps like many living animals (including frogs, squirrels and monkeys), small, feathered dinosaurs began to jump, glide and parachute from tree to tree, chasing prey or escaping from danger.

Archaeopteryx was discovered in Germany in rocks 150 million years old. Alongside its fossil bones are clear impressions of feathers forming two wings and a tail.

The Dodo lived on the island of Mauritius in the Indian Ocean. Because it could not fly it was easily hunted and became extinct by the end of the sixteenth century.

Q How could giants like dinosaurs have flown?

A *Tyrannosaurus rex* would never have got airborne! Some carnivorous dinosaurs though, like *Compsognathus* and *Ornitholestes*, were very small, lightly built with hollow bones and could run quickly. Perhaps they chased small lizards and insects and began to take to the air.

Q Are there any other fossil birds?

A Fossils of birds are very rare: their light hollow bones do not fossilise well. Examples that have been found include birds similar to large terns, ostriches, eagles and the Dodo.

Q Isn't a Pteranodon a flying dinosaur?

A No. Although they lived on Earth at the same time as the dinosaurs, *Pteranodons* belong to a group of flying reptiles, called pterosaurs.

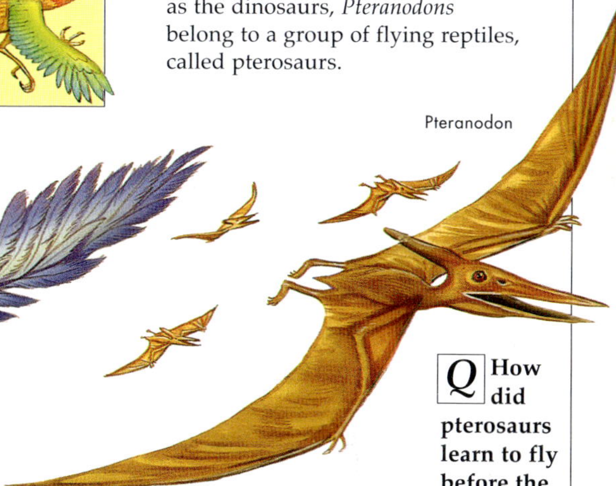

Pteranodon

Q How did pterosaurs learn to fly before the dinosaurs?

A The skeletons of the earliest known flying reptiles are similar to ancient carnivorous reptiles alive before the dinosaurs. Their skeletons were light and perhaps they too, like the later feathered dinosaurs, climbed trees and learnt to glide.

When dinosaur eggs are found, it is not always possible to say which dinosaur laid them.

Did dinosaurs have babies?

All living creatures reproduce and dinosaurs were no exception. It is believed that, like almost all living reptiles, dinosaurs laid eggs.

Q Have any fossil dinosaur eggs ever been found?

A Yes. The first ones found were discovered in the Gobi Desert of Mongolia, in 1921. They were neatly arranged in nests and were discovered with skeletons of the small horned dinosaur, *Protoceratops*.

Q Did all dinosaurs lay eggs?

A Fossil eggs have been found with sauropods, ceratopsians and a variety of other dinosaurs. However, they are very rare and the majority of dinosaurs have left no fossil eggs. But most scientists assume that all dinosaurs did lay eggs.

Q What do dinosaur eggs look like?

A Unlike most modern reptiles, dinosaurs seem to have laid eggs with hard shells. Eggs that have been found whole are usually oval-shaped, blunt at one end with a wrinkled surface. In the case of *Protoceratops*, they were about 20 cm long and laid in nests up to 30 or more at a time. Other eggs are usually between 120 and 170 mm long (as big as an ostrich egg).

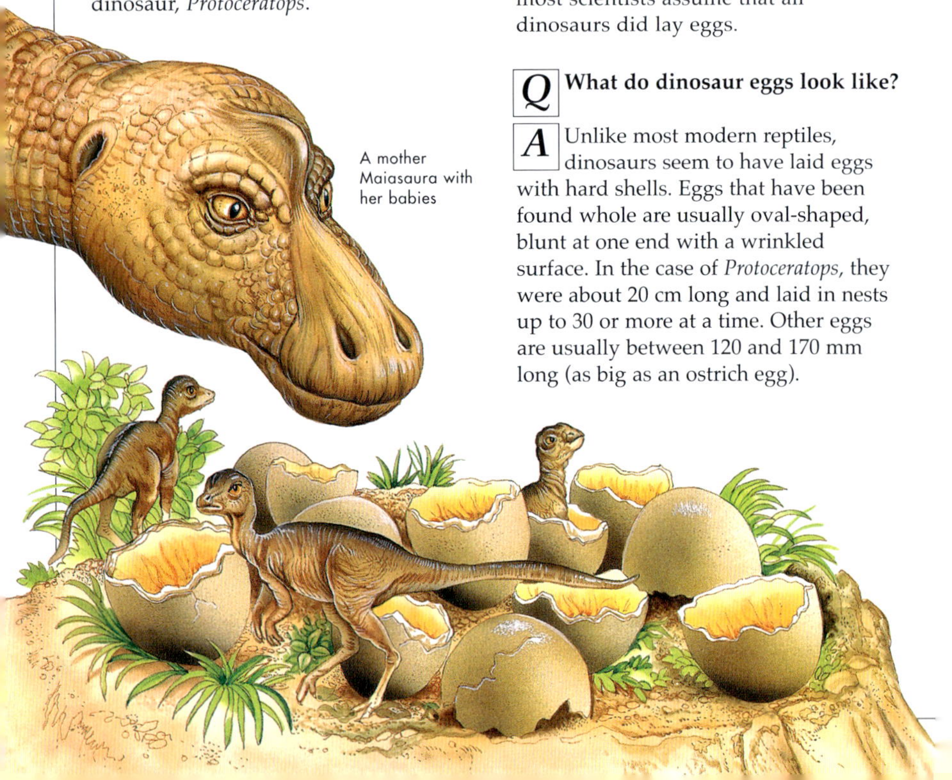

A mother Maiasaura with her babies

Eggs of the dinosaurs Orodromeus and Troodon, have been x-rayed and contain the tiny fossilised bones of embryos.

Some fossils of Chasmosaurus show that in herds, they formed a protective circle around their young to guard them from attack.

A herd of Chasmosaurus

Q Were dinosaurs good parents?

A Even the fiercest alligator living today is a very caring parent, feeding and protecting its young. The remains of *Maiasaura* dinochicks were found in Montana. Though their teeth show wear from eating, they were still in their nests. They were probably fed by their parents until they grew old enough to leave home.

Q How did young dinosaurs tell their mothers and fathers apart?

A Scientists can only guess whether a fossilised dinosaur is male or female. In a few examples where many skeletons have been found together, some are bigger than others - most likely the males where the bigger. We can be sure that baby dinosaurs knew the difference, even through behavioural differences.

Q Are there any fossils of baby dinosaurs?

A The smallest dinosaur skeleton is only 20 cm long - about the size of a blackbird. It has been called *Mussaurus* (mouse-lizard) but it is in fact a very young dinochick of a yet-unknown dinosaur. Other dinosaur babies found include *Protoceratops*, *Maiasaura*, *Psittacosaurus* and *Coelophysis*.

Baby Maiasaura

Q Did the gigantic sauropods lay gigantic eggs?

A The largest eggs found weighed 7 kg in weight - not much compared to 20 tonne sauropods!

Is this what Stenonychosaurus might have looked like if it had continued evolving?

Were dinosaurs stupid?

The original discoverers of *Apatosaurus* and *Diplodocus* were surprised at the small size of the heads compared to the bodies of the dinosaurs. They thought that with such small brains, the dinosaurs must have had little intelligence.

Q Which was the cleverest dinosaur?

A Size for size, *Stenonychosaurus* must have been the brightest dinosaur. Its brain is similar in proportion to birds and even some mammals, and much bigger than crocodiles.

Q Does a large brain mean that a dinosaur was clever?

A Brains control behaviour and the senses, as well as intelligence. The small carnivorous dinosaurs had large brains compared to the size of their bodies. As a result they had excellent vision, could move quickly and were good at learning how to hunt and catch their prey.

Stenonychosaurus

The brain of the Chinese stegosaur Tuojiangosaurus weighed only 70-80 grams.

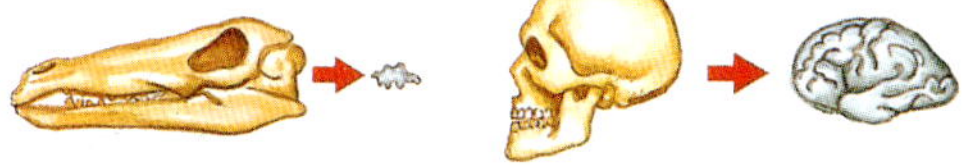

Q How big were dinosaur brains?

A For reptiles, most dinosaurs seem to have had quite large brains. The smaller, faster carnivores had the largest brains, though the largest of all was perhaps *Tyrannosaurus*. The stegosaurs had perhaps the smallest brains - about the size of a walnut!

Q How do you measure the brain of a dinosaur?

A Sometimes, when mud and sand surrounded a dinosaur skull after death, it filled the brain cavity too. The result - a fossil brain! Different areas of the brain can be seen as well as the bony passages for nerves and blood vessels.

Q Which dinosaurs were the least intelligent?

A The sauropods were the least intelligent. But however small their brains were, they were obviously good enough for them to survive as a group for 150 million years.

Q Did the enormous sauropods have enormous brains?

A Not necessarily so. Brains do not automatically get bigger in proportion to bodies. It depends on the dinosaur. The more active the dinosaur, the larger the brain needed to be to produce quicker reactions.

Q Do living reptiles have large brains?

A On average, crocodile and alligator brains are approximately the same size as similar sized dinosaurs. The brains of living mammals are ten times the size of similar sized living reptiles.

Some scientists believe that sauropod dinosaurs like Barosaurus might have had up to 8 hearts to help pump blood up their long necks.

How did their bodies work?

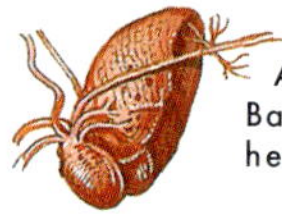

A Barosau heart.

The flesh and organs of all creatures rot away after death. To understand how the bodies of dinosaurs worked, scientists have to build up their ideas on very little evidence.

Q What did dinosaur blood look like?

A Like modern animals, dinosaurs needed blood to carry oxygen, heat and food around their bodies. Their blood was probably much the same as our own. To pump this blood, the dinosaurs needed hearts. Those of the biggest dinosaurs must have been enormous to pump blood to heads as high as 25 metres above the ground.

Q What was a dinosaur's normal body temperature?

A We will never know for sure. Reptiles today keep their bodies warm by lying in the sun. Cold weather can limit their movements. Most reptiles live in warm climates. Mammals and birds rely on their own bodies to release heat from food. If they were as active as we think they were dinosaurs may have been able to do th same thing. Once the biggest dinosa were warm, they would probably never have cooled down!

Barosaurus

Q Does fossil bone have fossil blood in it?

A Blood, unfortunately, does not fossilise, but some bony passages for blood vessels do. Microscopic studies of dinosaur bone have shown that it resembles the bone of living warm-blooded mammals, rather than the so-called cold-blooded living reptiles. This means that the dinosaurs may have been much more active than their living relatives.

Q How do we know what muscles dinosaurs had?

A Muscles are attached to bones. Because of this, bones carry scars of where the muscles were once fixed. The size and position of these marks on dinosaur bones allow scientists to reconstruct the shapes of legs, arms, hips and shoulders. Living reptiles also give some good clues.

Ouranosaurus had long spines running down its backbone. These would have been covered with skin to form a 'sail'. It could warm up and cool down by directing its sail towards or away from the sun.

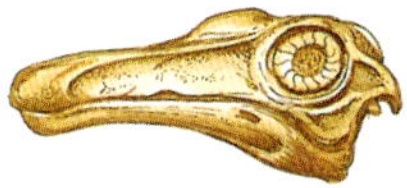

Gallimimus had very large eyes. Each eye was supported in its socket by a ring of bony plates which are often fossilised.

Ouranosaurus

Q How big were dinosaur ears?

A There is no evidence that any dinosaur had outer ears like elephants or even ourselves. Like modern reptiles and birds, dinosaur ears would probably have been visible on the surface of their heads. They would look like circular marks in the skin.

The nostrils of the duck-bill dinosaur called *Saurolophus* are thought to have been covered by an inflatable pouch of skin. Perhaps like many birds, Saurolophus could blow this up into a large, colourful balloon to warn off rivals or to signal to the opposite sex.

Q How did dinosaurs smell?

A Dinosaurs had holes in their skulls for the nostrils to allow for breathing. They probably used them for smelling too. Some dinosaurs like *Camarasaurus* had very large nostrils on top of the head. Scientists once thought that these helped the dinosaurs to breathe underwater.

Q What colour were dinosaurs' eyes?

A We will never know the answer, but the eyes of living reptiles are usually bright and yellow. They are not surrounded by white like our own. Scientists can tell from dinosaur skulls that most had large eyes and so could probably see very well.

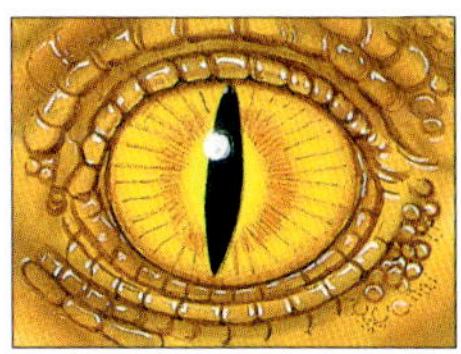

Some scientists believe that less than 10 per cent of dinosaur types that ever existed have been found fossilised.

How do you find a dinosaur?

Fossils are found in rocks formed from mud and sand left by water or wind. They are called sedimentary rocks. Identifying what age rocks belong to is a good start to finding dinosaurs.

Q How do dinosaurs turn into fossils?

A

Q How do they know if the rocks are old enough to contain dinosaur fossils?

A All sorts of plants and animals lived with the dinosaurs and their fossils are much more common: ferns, snails, freshwater fish, shellfish and even insects. Recognising the right type of rocks with the right type of fossils shows that dinosaurs might be around.

Q How do scientists know where to look for a dinosaur?

A The most common fossils are found in rocks formed under water, especially the seas or oceans. Dinosaurs only lived on the land and so are not so common. They are found in rocks that formed near rivers, lakes, seashores and also deserts.

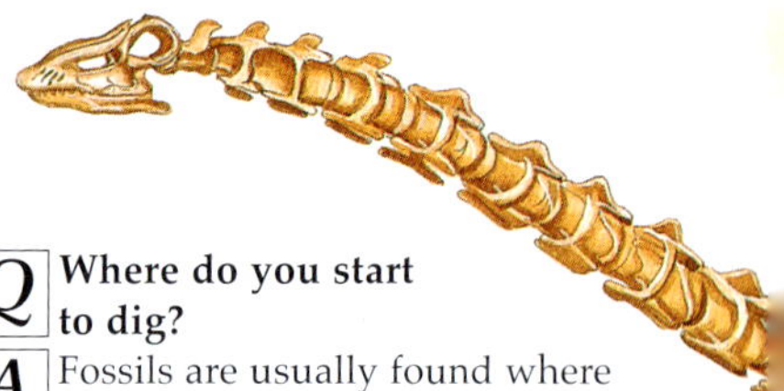

Q Where do you start to dig?

A Fossils are usually found where the rocks can be seen - quarries, cliffs or mountains. Fossil hunters then hunt for odd bones sticking out of the rock, made visible by wind and rain. *Baryonyx* was discovered by a man who found only a single claw in a busy quarry. Most of the skeleton was found later by expert excavation.

Some of the dinosaur fossils found early this century have still not been fully extracted from the rock in which they were collected.

Before dinosaur bones are removed from an excavation they are cocooned in plaster of paris or foam jackets to protect them on the journey back to the laboratory.

Q How do you dig up a dinosaur?

A Excavating a dinosaur is not an easy job! After discovery, several tons of rock might need to be moved by diggers, bulldozers and pneumatic drills. Hammers and chisels might be used for more careful work before a bone can be removed.

Q What do you do with a dinosaur once it has been dug up?

A Bones may be cracked and only partly visible in their enclosing rock. They are taken to laboratories where the rock is carefully removed with special tools and cracks are constantly repaired. It may be years before all the bones are prepared. Only if the bones are in very good condition might they be joined to make a skeleton.

Q Are there any dinosaurs left to find?

A Though it is very rare to find a completely new dinosaur, *Baryonyx* is a dinosaur unlike any other, and it was found in 1982. In Canada, millions of dinosaur bones can be seen scattered in Dinosaur Provincial Park: three or four complete skeletons are found each year.

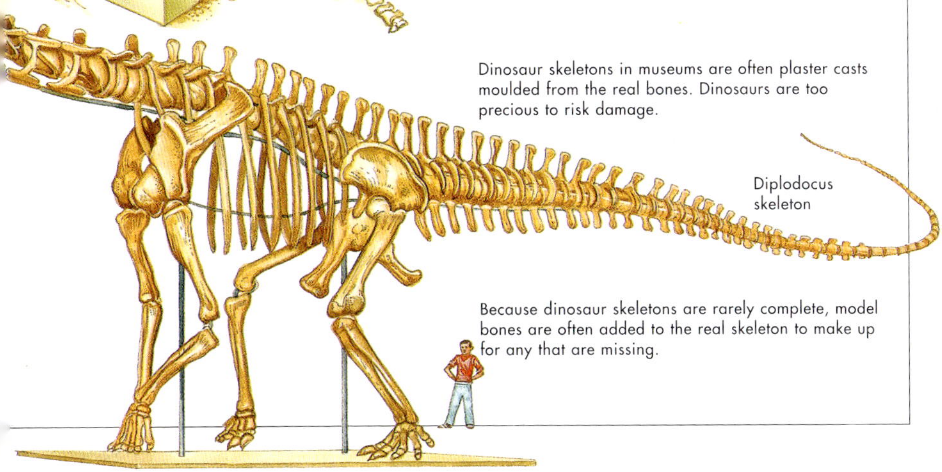

Dinosaur skeletons in museums are often plaster casts moulded from the real bones. Dinosaurs are too precious to risk damage.

Because dinosaur skeletons are rarely complete, model bones are often added to the real skeleton to make up for any that are missing.

How do you become an expert?

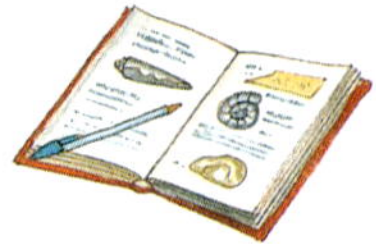

You can collect dinosaur models, toys, games and postage stamps from around the world.

The study of fossils is called palaeontology 'old-life study'. Many years of learning are needed to become a palaeontologist, but there are lots of ways to become interested in dinosaurs.

Make a catalogue in an exercise book to help you remember what the fossils are and what you know about them.

Q What do you have to study at school to become a dinosaur expert?

A All fossils are the remains of once living creatures so biology is important. Mathematics and English will always be useful and later, physics and chemistry.

Q Can you learn about dinosaurs at university?

A There are no courses specifically about dinosaurs. At university you learn about different aspects of geology - rocks, minerals and fossils, and the processes that have made and shaped the Earth. You could also study zoology and learn about living animals before specialising in dinosaur studies.

Q How can I find dinosaur fossils?

A It helps if you live in an area where dinosaur fossils are known to occur but you would still have to be very lucky. The commonest dinosaur finds are probably teeth. Start by making a collection of other fossils to get experience. Leaflets and books may be found in libraries, shops and museums.

The first dinosaur skeleton to be put together was an Iguanodon from Belgium. It was assembled in 1882. The bones were hung from scaffolding by ropes so that they could be moved until they looked right. Then they were supported by an iron frame.

Q What do I need to look for fossils?

A A hammer and chisel are useful to split open rocks. Protective clothing is needed too - gloves for hammering, goggles to guard your eyes and a hard hat to protect your head, especially near cliffs.

Q What do I do if I find a fossil?

A Remove the fossil carefully and wrap it in kitchen roll or toilet tissue. Make a note of where and when you found it. At home, clean away loose dirt with a dry brush. If this does not work, try brushing with a little water. When the fossil is dry write a number on it for use in a catalogue of your finds. Store your fossil safely by making a tissue 'nest' for it in a box or drawer.

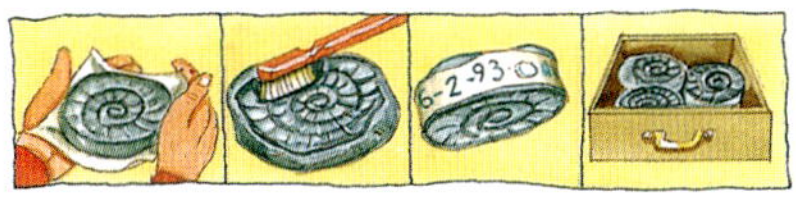

Model-makers and artists must work closely with palaeontologists if their models and pictures are to look right. Muscles are carefully drawn onto a skeleton outline and the skin added so that the basic shape is right.

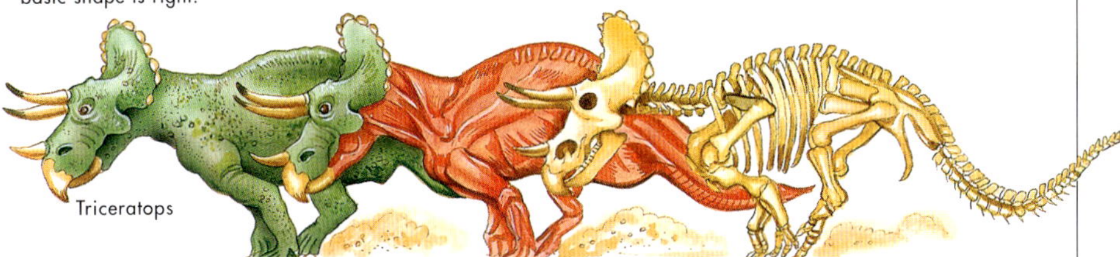

Triceratops

Q What tips are there for collecting fossils?

A Never collect without the permission of the landowner.

Never collect from cliffs or quarry walls. It is much safer to work on fallen blocks or waste tips.

Do not be greedy - leave some fossils for others to find.

Replace your poorer fossils when you find better examples.

Q Can I get any help?

A Visit your local museum and ask if there is a geologist on the staff. If you have collected fossils someone may help you to identify them. You may also be able to find out if there is a local geological society. Society members will include many enthusiastic collectors. Find out from them about the latest information on dinosaurs.

A popular theory for the death of the dinosaurs is that a meteorite 6-15 km in diameter hit the Earth.

What happened to dinosaurs?

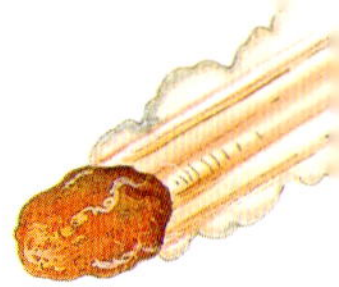

There are no dinosaurs alive today. One of the great mysteries in the history of life on Earth is why such a successful group of animals should become extinct.

Q When did the dinosaurs become extinct?

A Rocks about 70 million years old, from all over the world, contain dinosaur fossils. Amazingly, only 5 or 6 million years later, not a single dinosaur had survived.

Q What was the last type of dinosaur to live?

A It is not always easy to tell whether rocks in one place on Earth are a little bit younger or older than rocks in other places. So, we are not sure if some dinosaurs outlived others thousands of miles away. Certainly the last dinosaur groups included *Tyrannosaurus* and *Triceratops*. A bone-head dinosaur (pachycephalosaur) called *Stygimoloch* from Montana, USA may have been the very last to survive - but only a few pieces of broken skull have been found.

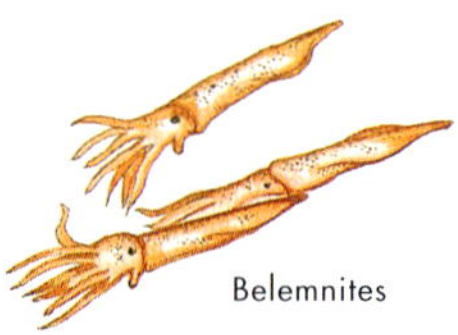

Belemnites

Ammonite

Q What could have caused the dinosaurs to die out?

A Possible explanations for dinosaur extinction:

Funny	Mistakes	Serious
Boredom - after 150 million years.	Constipation from the new flowering plants.	Competition from the mammals.
Only male or female dinosaurs left.	Eggs eaten by the mammals.	Climate getting colder.
Too much smoking.	Disease from a new virus.	Brains got smaller.
New caterpillars ate all the leaves.	Holes in the ozone layer caused by radiation.	High temperatures caused by a meteorite explosion.

Q What else became extinct with the dinosaurs?

A All the large marine reptiles - the mosasaurs and plesiosaurs, as well as the flying reptiles, disappeared. Also some types of shellfish, including the ammonites and belemnites, and huge numbers of microscopic marine plants vanished.

Iridium, a common element in meterorites, has been found worldwide in rocks of the same age.

In Mexico, fossil tree trunks have been found mixed up with rocks from the ocean floor. These are evidence of the huge tidal waves that a large meteorite would cause.

Q What survived the great extinction?

A The majority of plants and animals survived. These included the other reptiles such as snakes, lizards, crocodiles and turtles. Birds and the early mammals survived too, together with shellfish, corals, starfish, insects and land plants.

Q What do scientists think is the real reason dinosaurs died out?

A Most scientists now agree that two things caused the death of the dinosaurs and many other creatures. First, the climate had been gradually cooling down. Second, around 64 million years ago, something catastrophic happened. Some people believe a huge meteriorite struck the Earth.

Map of Mexico showing likely area of meteorite impact.

Q How could a meteorite do so much damage?

A A large meteorite hitting the Earth would throw up a gigantic cloud of dust. This would cut out sunlight for months, perhaps years causing plants and animals to die. Some, like the dinosaurs, never recovered.

Q Is it possible that dinosaurs are alive somewhere on Earth?

A Sadly, though there are occasional stories and legends, no-one seriously believes that even a small dinosaur could have remained undetected. But dinosaur descendents are still all around us in the form of birds.

Index